DAUGHTER, COME HOME

Restoring the Daughter's Heart to a Loving Father
Devotional Journal

JODIANNA R. CLARKE

DAYELight
PUBLISHERS

ISBN: 978-1-966723-33-2 (paperback)

Scripture quotations marked "KJV" are taken from the Holy Bible, King James Version (Public Domain).

Scripture quotations marked (NIV) are taken from the Holy Bible, New International Version®, NIV®. Copyright © 1973, 1978, 1984 by Biblica, Inc.™ Used by permission of Zondervan. All rights reserved worldwide.

Scripture quotations marked "NASB" are taken from the New American Standard Bible®, Copyright © 1960, 1962, 1963, 1968, 1971, 1972, 1973, 1975, 1977, 1995 by The Lockman Foundation. Used by permission.

Scripture quotations marked (NLT) are taken from the Holy Bible, New Living Translation, copyright © 1996, 2004, 2007 by Tyndale House Foundation. Used by permission of Tyndale House Publishers, Inc., Carol Stream, Illinois 60188. All rights reserved.

Scripture quotations marked "NKJV" are taken from the New King James Version. Copyright © 1982 by Thomas Nelson, Inc. Used by permission. All rights reserved. Bible text from the New King James Version® is not to be reproduced in copies or otherwise by any means except as permitted in writing by Thomas Nelson, Inc., Attn: Bible Rights and Permissions, P.O. Box 141000, Nashville, TN 37214-1000.

Scripture quotations marked "ESV" are from the ESV Bible® (The Holy Bible, English Standard Version®), copyright © 2001 by Crossway Bibles, a publishing ministry of Good News Publishers. Used by permission. All rights reserved.

Scripture quotations taken from the Amplified® Bible (AMP). Copyright © 2015 by The Lockman Foundation. Used by permission. www.Lockman.org.

Scripture quotations taken from the Amplified® Bible Classic. Copyright © 1954, 1958, 1962, 1964, 1965, 1987 by The Lockman Foundation. Used by permission. (www.Lockman.org).

Scriptures Quotations marked "GNB" or "GNT" are from the Good News Bible © 1994 published by the Bible Societies/HarperCollins Publishers Ltd UK, Good News Bible © American Bible Society 1966, 1971, 1976, 1992. Used with permission.

Scripture quotations marked (ERV) are taken from the Holy Bible: Easy-to-Read Version (ERV), International Edition © 2013, 2016 by Bible League International and used by permission.

DEDICATION

This book is for every daughter whose love for her Father has grown cold and for every woman who has carried the weight of the world alone. My prayer is that you find rest, renewal, and the reminder that you are never forgotten.

To my sisters, **Sasha-Gaye, Sashaunna, and Roxanne**—may we always hold fast to the truth that we are daughters of the King.

ACKNOWLEDGMENTS

I stop to thank God for the gift of restoration and for a heart that calls His daughters back home.

This book would not have been possible without the love and unwavering support of so many special people:

- **Sade Powell, Zonya Pryce and Gayon Williams Dalley** – my fearless cheerleaders and dear friends, thank you for always believing in me.

- **Transformed Life Church** – for being the place where God truly transforms lives and where I experienced His restoring power.

- **Pastor Tania Case** – you are the hands God used to guide me back home, and I am forever grateful.

- **Crystal Daye** – thank you for helping me shape this vision into a book and walking with me through the process.

- **Patrick and Beverley Clarke** – for nurturing my love of words and planting seeds that continue to grow through this work.

To each of you, I am deeply thankful. This journey would not have been the same without you.

TABLE OF CONTENTS

Week 1

Where Are You?

Week 2

The Father's Heart

Week 3

Journey to the Father

Preparing For The Journey

Your Father bids you—come home.

If you have taken the time to invest in reading this book, thank you. Thank you for answering the silent nudge of the Holy Spirit to spend time with you, for listening to the loud thud in your soul crying out for more.

I wrote this book for you. I wrote this book for me. This book flows out of my own journey back to the Father's heart and to a place of peace and identity.

He called me daughter, but I felt and lived outside of that reality.

Over the next fifteen days, we will go on an interesting journey backpacking across the stories and extracting truth—truth of where we are, truth of who God is as our Father, and ultimately the truth of restoring our identity as daughters in Him.

To make the most of this journey, there are a few things we need to pack:

1. Time

Yes, I encourage you to make time to read, re-read, and listen. God is speaking, but it sometimes takes lingering in His presence to hear the message within the message.

2. Bible

I tried my best to insert as many of the scriptures used as best as possible, but I still encourage you to grab your Bible.

3. Pretty Stationery and Journal

Yes, grab your most beautiful journal, colored pens, and highlighters. This devotional includes activation questions at the end, which I encourage you to take your time answering. Each week has only five days outlined, and the remaining two days are to spend time reviewing the activation question(s) and making detailed notes.

4. Prayer

Our final piece to pack for the journey is a heart willing to talk to God—to invite Him into the parts of your story that are still painful and unhealed. He longs to talk to you.

With our bags packed, let us start on our journey to our loving Father.

WEEK 1

WHERE ARE YOU?

Where can I go from Your Spirit?
Or where can I flee from Your presence?
If I ascend to heaven, You are there;
If I make my bed in Sheol (the nether world, the place of the dead), behold, You
are there.
If I take the wings of the dawn,
If I dwell in the remotest part of the sea,
Even there Your hand will lead me,
And Your right hand will take hold of me. (Psalm 139:7-10 – AMP).

Over the next five days, we will spend some time with our sisters in the Bible. We will uncover their stories and hold them up as a small flashlight shining light into our own stories, set against the question asked to Eve from the dawn of time.

Where are you?

Grab your backpack and let's go!

Where Are You?

Silenced

TODAY'S READING: 2 SAMUEL 13

I was sitting at Trumpet Call Ministry International Women's Encounter 2024, wondering why I was there. Why did God take me back to a place where I had so much joy, so much community, but so much pain and regret? I had no idea what God was up to. As I sat listening to one of the day's presenters, I sat in awe to see her preach the Word with such power and passion. As she went through her session, she would eventually lead me to the answer to why I was there.

She introduced me to Tamar.

TAMAR

Born of noble blood, daughter to King David.
Dressed in royal robes reserved for the king's virgin daughters.
Desired for her beauty, trapped by her lustful half-brother.
Raped. Discarded. Disgraced.
In the end, silenced and desolate.

This week, as we go through the various places we have found ourselves on this journey called life, we start with the powerful yet painful story of Tamar, daughter of King David. I encourage you to pause here and read 2 Samuel 13:1-20 to get a full understanding of Tamar's story before we go deeper.

Tamar's story paints for us a vivid picture of the trauma and injustice that can silence our voices. Though some of us may not have been raped like Tamar, our royal garments were still destroyed. When we put it into context, royal garments signify our royal status and are a sign of our direct connection to the King as a daughter. The ripping of our royal robes by others or by our mistakes has led many of us to wrap ourselves in ashes and waste away in pain that has become our prison.

As I sat in what was usually a cool room at Teamwork Christian Center, I felt a slight rumbling in my spirit as the presenter looked at the women in the room. *"Tamar was never heard from again… she was never heard from again."* I could feel the room slowly get smaller as the question barreled towards the truth of my condition. *Have I been silenced?*

Though my story differs from Tamar's, I can clearly remember the moments when my own decisions led me to strip off my royal robes and take up the ashes of shame. As our presenter went through the definition of desolation, which is *a state of complete emptiness or destruction*, she pointed out that though that was Tamar's story, it doesn't have to be ours. But thanks to Tamar, my eyes to my own position in God were painfully opened as the Word brought light.

The unfolding of your words gives light; it imparts understanding to the simple. (Psalm 119:130 – ESV).

Light came and hit me like a lightning bolt.

13

THE COST OF SILENCE

My curiosity about Tamar's story outlived the Encounter weekend, as her story served as a mirror of one of the many ways we are silenced as daughters of the King. Using the symbol of the cross, let us look at two ways being silenced can impact us:

1. Our communication *with* our Father (upward).

Every relationship requires consistent communication, and when broken by trauma of any kind, it requires deliberate, intentional effort to repair. In Jamaican lingo, we would ask *"Yu malice God?* or *"Yu ave up God inna yu heart?"* When we look at Tamar, it was her brother who asked her to be quiet.

Can you identify who silenced you? At what point did that passion for God, the Father, run dry and get cold? Let us also take a moment to pause and admit that many of us became silent from the decisions we made and the paths we chose to take.

To identify if we have been silenced, I invite us to answer these questions in our journals honestly:

- How consistently do I pray?
- How active is my devotional life?
- How clearly and consistently do I hear God's voice each day?

2. Our communication *about* our Father (outward).

Another area where we are often silenced is in how we talk about our Father. As a proud Daddy's girl, I have noticed something about a daughter who is confident about her earthly father's love and protection. She moves confidently in the world and boasts easily about her identity as a daughter. Let us examine the way we talk about our heavenly Father by answering these questions in our journals.

- Are we sharing our faith boldly and inviting others to join us?

- Are we actively involved in the area of ministry we are called to serve?

- Are we plugged into a kingdom ministry that is advancing the gospel throughout the world?

ABSALOM'S HOUSE

As we close our time together today, let's talk briefly about Absalom's house.

Her brother Absalom said to her, "Has that Amnon, your brother, been with you? Be quiet for now, my sister; he is your brother. Don't take this thing to heart." And Tamar lived in her brother Absalom's house, a desolate woman. (2 Samuel 13:20 – AMP).

Absalom's house is the place where our silence has grown into desolation, where we have been locked away or confined. For us, Absalom's house may not be physical, but it may be our broken heart, trauma, or den of negative thoughts. For me, it was the shame of the mistakes I had made, despite God's warning to trust Him and to wait. My inability to forgive myself became my Absalom's house. I was a captive in the pain of my past, and the longer I stayed there, the more comfortable I became with being voiceless and fading out of purpose. I thank God for what was done that day at Women's Encounter, and today I hope to do it for you.

Tamar was never heard from again; being raped and shut up in Absalom's house ruined her chances at the future she may have been destined to have, but that is not our story.

For all my sisters who were taken advantage of by people who were called to protect you, we pray God's swift justice and a baptism of love on your behalf.

Absalom's home is not the end. We reclaim our voice.

ACTIVATION #1

My heart told me to come to you, LORD, so I am coming to ask for your help. (Psalm 27:8 - ERV).

Even if you have not prayed in a while, with sincerity, ask the Holy Spirit to explore these questions with you as you journal your responses.

1. Have you been silenced in any area of your life?

2. Ask the Holy Spirit to show you where you lost your voice.

3. Ask Him to reveal what represents the house of Absalom in your life.

Where Are You?

Hiding

TODAY'S READING: GENESIS 3

"God says you are to come out of hiding; He is calling you out of the shadows."

As Nickeisha Austin held my hand on New Year's Eve 2023, the tears rolled down my face as she prayed. This was the second time God had sent the same prophetic word through different people. The problem was that the shadows had become my friend; I enjoyed being hidden.

Today, we spend some time with Eve, and yes, we lay a lot of blame at her feet, but did you realize that it was in Eve's story that we see the first model of the Father-daughter dynamic? You see, Eve was the first of her kind, hewn from the rib of a man who was put asleep while her Father chiseled and formed her beauty and grit. Unlike everything else around, she wasn't spoken into being like light or created from the dust like man.

Eve was formed—intimately and intentionally.

So the LORD God caused a deep sleep to fall upon the man, and while he slept took one of his ribs and closed up its place with flesh. And the rib that the LORD God had taken from the man he made into a woman and brought her to the man. (Genesis 2:21-22 - ESV).

From these two verses, we learn a fundamental truth that I hope will resonate with you today.

GOD'S DAUGHTER

You are God's daughter
Formed in His hand
Carved from the raw material of the strongest bones
Presented as an expression of His love to the world
Before you were known to the world
You were known by Him
You are His masterpiece.

THE QUESTION

The question is, *How did we move from Eve being formed intricately by her Father to her covering herself with fig leaves?* As we join Eve in the Garden in Genesis 3, we see her engaging in a conversation with the enemy of her soul. He started with a question that we are going to meditate on today.

Now the serpent was more crafty than any other beast of the field that the LORD God had made. He said to the woman, **"Did God actually say, 'You shall not eat of any tree in the garden?'"** *(Genesis 3:1 - ESV – emphasis mine).*

DID GOD REALLY SAY?

Did God really say you are the head and not the tail?
Did God really say your land would be married?
Did God really say none among you would be barren?
Did God really say He would bless your food and water?

For me, my desire for marriage was my **"Did God really say…"** moment. *What is yours?*

This is an area where I consistently fell short, as I never fully accepted God's truth about myself and acknowledged that His plans for my future were good. Let me be honest, in my twenties, I looked around in the kingdom and didn't like what I saw in terms of potential husbands, so I went with what looked good to me. Like Eve, I saw that the tree was good for fruit, and it was pleasing to the eye, and I ate of it. This led to years of bad relationships and choices that drew me further away from the Father's hand. I open my story to you only to let you know that you are not alone in following a desire that led to a breakdown in your relationship with the Father. If you are reading this devotional, you are most likely a daughter who is joining me on the journey of making our way back home.

That seed of **"Did God really say…"** will land on any area of unbelief within our souls, and if pondered on long enough, will germinate and bear fruit with long-lasting consequences. As we see with Eve, what started as a question planted by the enemy led to her ultimate deception and separation from God.

OUR RESPONSE

Then the eyes of both were opened, and they knew that they were naked. And they sewed fig leaves together and made themselves loincloth. And they heard the sound of the LORD God walking in the garden in the cool of the day, and the man and his wife hid themselves from the presence of the LORD God among the trees of the garden. (Genesis 3:7-8 – ESV).

But the story of Eve has many parallels with our own, as Eve's actions once her eyes were opened are truly symbolic of what many of us have done once we realize we have been deceived.

1. Sewing fig leaves together to cover areas of deep pain.

Through outward success in other areas, we have made fig leaves to cover the breakdown of our relationship with our Father. We have married well and had beautiful children. We have amazing careers that fund the acquisition of material assets. We have climbed the corporate ladder and become real influencers in the world. Many of us have busied ourselves in ministry, serving a God with whom we have no relationship. The covering of our wounds with fig leaves covers the deep wounds of our souls.

2. Hiding from God's presence.

God in His holiness cannot tolerate sin, and once we become aware of our own nakedness and failure, it is a natural reaction in the face of a holy God to run away. Pastor Sarah Jakes Robert has always famously said that Eve knew better but didn't do better. This is true of many of us, and that awareness has led some of us to live in permanent hiding.

3. Hiding among the trees of the garden.

The Bible says they hid among the trees. We see Adam and Eve attempting to blend into what they were called to rule over and govern. Many of us are hiding among the world so that we will not be seen. We have quieted our passion for our Father because the shame of coming back to Him is too much.

GOD'S RESPONSE

Today, as we close, can you identify:

- What area has caused a separation between you and the Father?

- What fig leaves have been used to cover those areas?

At the end of Genesis 3, there are some lessons from this powerful encounter between Eve and her Father that I want to leave you with today.

The LORD God said to the serpent, "Because you have done this, cursed are you above all livestock and above all beasts of the field; on your belly you shall go, and dust you shall eat all the days of your life. I will put enmity between you and the woman, and between your offspring and her offspring; he shall bruise your head, and you shall bruise his heel." (Genesis 3:14-15 - ESV).

1. God initiated reconciliation.

Genesis 3:8 shows us that God came to the place of their usual meeting, and they were not there. It was God who asked, *"Where are you?"* It can be very hard to picture that the God of the universe will notice that you are missing from His presence, that the relationship has gone cold, and that His daughter is in hiding. At the same time, reconciliation needs two parties, and we have a critical role to play. Eve was honest when God asked her what had happened. She owned up to eating the fruit. It can be hard when filled with regret to make our way back to the Father with honesty and openness about our mistakes. Hiding feels safer, but it is not. As you read this devotional, may you feel Him tugging on your heart to come out of hiding and into His love.

2. God dealt with Eve's enemy.

Though Eve fell into deception and was separated from her Father, upon her confession of her sin, He arose in His role of protector and eternally judged her enemy. Our Father is ready to deal with the enemy that has deceived and robbed us of a deep relationship with Him. We cannot defeat the enemy behind the fig leaves alone; our Father is ready to dispatch angel armies on our behalf.

3. God revealed Eve's greater purpose as mother.

God, the Father, fashioned Eve out of Adam's need for help; she was created as a solution. However, in Genesis 3, after the fall, we see God, in meting out His judgment for their disobedience, giving Eve a further glimpse into her purpose. God revealed that Eve would be a mother and her offspring would crush the head of the enemy. After what seemed like her greatest defeat, God revealed her greatest purpose. He is ready to do the same for you today.

Did you know that up to this point, Eve was not named? She was referred to as "woman" or "wife." In Genesis 3:20, we see Adam naming her "Eve" because she would become the mother of all living. A chapter that started with deception and pain ended with a release of great purpose.

Your greatest victory awaits. Take off the fig leaves and come out of hiding.

ACTIVATION #2

As you spend some time with God and your journal, ask the Holy Spirit to give you courage to answer the following:

1. What promise from God are you struggling to believe?

2. Do you see an attack from the enemy in that area?

3. What fig leaves have you used to cover the pain of your past decisions?

4. Ask God how purpose will emerge from this place of pain, and take the fig leaves off.

Where Are You?

Cringing In Accusation

TODAY'S READING: JOHN 8:1-11

I still remember it clearly, even after seven years of not attending that church or being in the same city. I recall sitting in my then-pastor's office and explaining why I could no longer serve as a youth leader. I recall walking her through my moral failures, feeling the deep grip of shame envelop me. It was an experience that, to this day, has made me cautious about entering any ministry. It made me almost not write this book. Today, we are hanging out in the story of an unlikely woman—the woman caught in adultery. I remember my own moment and wondered how she must have felt as the Pharisees dragged her in front of Jesus and the crowd He was teaching.

Let's read this short account we find in John 8:1-11:

but Jesus went to the Mount of Olives. Early in the morning he came again to the temple. All the people came to him, and he sat down and taught them. The scribes and the Pharisees brought a woman who had been caught in adultery, and placing her in the midst they said to him, "Teacher, this woman has been caught in the act of adultery. Now in the Law, Moses commanded us to stone such women. So what do you say?" This they said to test him, that they might have some charge to bring against him. Jesus bent down and wrote with his finger on the ground. And as they continued to ask him, he stood up and said to them, "Let him who is without sin among you be the first to throw a stone at her." And once more he bent down and wrote on the ground. But when they heard it, they went away one by one, beginning with the older ones, and Jesus was left alone with the woman standing before him. Jesus stood up and said to her, "Woman, where are they? Has no one condemned you?" She said, "No one, Lord." And Jesus said, "Neither do I condemn you; go, and from now on sin no more." (ESV).

As I read this story, I picture a woman dragged out of bed, barely covered, possibly barefoot, hair disheveled, and placed before a man who claims He is the Son of God. I picture her heart racing as she tries to maintain some dignity with a crowd of eyes piercing her skin with accusation. She was cringing with her hands protecting her head as she got ready to be stoned, to face sudden death as prescribed by the law. After all, she was guilty!

Today, please silence your thoughts and identify the voices that have run rampant in your own life. Is it fear, hopelessness, childhood abuse, and molestation? Has failure held up its stone to clobber you if you dare take a step of faith? A few of the voices that can be the loudest are the mistakes of our past, the words of our childhood, and the whispers of our dreams. Like a tug-of-war, these voices are constantly in a battle for our attention.

In the story, there are a few things I want to focus on, and I urge you to see them with fresh eyes.

- **A woman was dragged before Jesus by the religious rulers who were ready to stone her.**

The woman caught was found guilty of a sin that made her immediately eligible to be stoned, and she must have known this. Imagine the terror and dread she felt, being found out by the religious leaders and knowing her fate immediately. We have no idea why or how she was caught; all we know is that everyone saw her as guilty.

What verdict has our sin pronounced over us? The truth is, whether we are exposed or not, we have an enemy called the accuser of the brethren. Has he called you backslider, fornicator, thief, gossiper, and are they playing on repeat in your own head and emotions? When we level the playing field, we all have something that makes us worthy of being dragged before Jesus.

- **A silent Jesus writing in the dirt.**

Jesus' silence when first approached may be construed as Him not caring or being too slow to respond. How many times have we felt that way, like He has abandoned us when the voice of our accuser was breathing down our necks? Jesus took a different position; He remained silent but stooped down to write in the dirt. This carries for us a very powerful lesson; His silence is not an indication of His absence. As the story moves on, we realize that what was written in the dirt was powerful enough to have her accusers hold their tongues and drop their stones.

- **A woman spared from stoning but caused to face her sin.**

Here we have a guilty woman; she was caught in her sin and deserved the penalty of stoning. Jesus stepped in and saved her, but He did not just wish her well. He asked her no questions but gave her one of the most critical instructions: *"Go thy way and sin no more."* Let's look at possible reasons for this charge to her and to us today.

SIN NO MORE

1. Sin, whether private or public, opens us up to accusation.

The enemy of our soul is real and is described as a prowling lion seeking whom he may devour (see 1 Peter 5:8). He is also described in Revelation 12:9-12b as *"the accuser of our brethren…cast down, which accused them before our God day and night."* (KJV). Sin gives the enemy a legal foothold to accuse and attack us in various ways. Many of us have been stuck under the sting of accusation and are constantly on the defensive and unable to live freely.

2. There is a call to sin no more.

It is easy to read this story and miss the most important part. Though it is painful what happened to the woman caught in adultery, it set her up for a one-on-one encounter with the only Man with the ability to save her from her sin. In a very direct way, Jesus deals with the issue, telling her, *"Go thy way and sin no more."* As a loving Father, He does not overlook the true issue at hand—sin. Though sending her on her way, He calls her up to a higher standard, as He does with all of us, as He rescues us from the onslaught of the enemy. His call to her was simple, and the call to us is the same: *Sin no more.* Sin separates us from the Father and from truly growing in our calling as daughters of the King. Though just three simple words, that command echoes throughout centuries and into our hearts today.

Let's take a quick look at Peter's story and the charge that God gave to him before he denied Jesus.

27

"Simon, Simon, Satan has asked to sift each of you like wheat. But I have pleaded in prayer for you, Simon, that your faith should not fail. So when you have repented and turned to me again, strengthen your brothers." (Luke 22:31-32 – NLT).

This text precedes Peter's denial of Jesus as He is being put on trial. I bring this in to show you that God is not shocked by your sin, no matter how severe you may think it is. There is a purpose in your restoration. Though the voice of accusation and guilt led Judas to suicide, Peter was fueled to be the greatest evangelist. Jesus told Peter, even before his sin, that after he "turned back," after he repented, when he got back into alignment, he was to strengthen his brothers. Whether it be from the enemy or our own community, the voice of accusation makes us doubt the voice of God, the love of God, and discourages us from stepping out. But what makes this verse powerful is that Jesus acknowledges Simon Peter's sin, not in condemnation, but in giving him a mandate to fulfill.

The mandate is the same for you.

There is a purpose assigned to your restoration. Today, I encourage you, as a fellow daughter on the journey back to our Father, to radically deal with the areas of your life that have kept you away from your Father. May the grace of God sovereignly silence the voice of the accuser as you see Jesus arise as your Advocate.

ACTIVATION #3

Prayerfully complete the questions in your journal as you reflect and answer the questions.

1. Is there an area where voices of accusation have held you bound?

2. Have you faced negative labels at home, work, or church that you feel trapped by?

3. Recall an area of guilt where Jesus stood up for you.

Where Are You?

Thriving In The Palace

TODAY'S READING: ESTHER 2

When I shared the outline for section 1 of this book with my friend, Sade, her eyes were drawn to Esther as a character I would be looking at. I too found it odd that God would highlight Esther as an example that we could learn from as we make our way back to Him. He then began a beautiful journey of unveiling how our work, careers, or chosen professions become places where we often hide and find identities outside of Him. He began to show me that, in a season when I had walked away from the community of a local church, it was the career and community I built at work that fueled my life. God further revealed that, though He had used my job as an avenue to bless me, He had also sent me there with a clear purpose. Today, we spend some time with Queen Esther; her rise to the position of Queen, and her ultimate choice to confront an enemy found in her court.

Esther 1 starts by setting the context of the book. We meet a successful King Xerxes basking in his wealth, an extravagant display that lasted 180 days, during which the alcohol flowed freely. This was followed by 7 days in his enclosed gardens, where all his people were invited to participate. Esther 1:10-12 brings us to the key point in the story that sets the stage for the rest of the book to unfold. Let's read:

On the seventh day, when King Xerxes was in high spirits from wine, he commanded the seven eunuchs who served him—Mehuman, Biztha, Harbona, Bigtha, Abagtha, Zethar and Karkas—to bring before him Queen Vashti, wearing her royal crown, in order to display her beauty to the people and nobles, for she was lovely to look at. But when the attendants delivered the king's command, Queen Vashti refused to come. Then the king became furious and burned with anger. (NIV).

Vashti's refusal to parade in front of her drunk husband and the kingdom has been a topic of debate for as long as I can remember. Many laud her for taking a stand and maintaining her integrity as a woman and a Queen, while others view her refusal as a dishonor to her husband and king, deserving of the punishment she faced. But this decision by Queen Vashti prompted the search for a new queen among the virgins of the land.

When the king's order and edict had been proclaimed, many young women were brought to the citadel of Susa and put under the care of Hegai. Esther also was taken to the king's palace and entrusted to Hegai, who had charge of the harem. She pleased him and won his favor. Immediately he provided her with her beauty treatments and special food. He assigned to her seven female attendants selected from the king's palace and moved her and her attendants into the best place in the harem. (Esther 2: 8-9 – NIV).

Before we continue the story, I would like us to reflect on our own journeys and the successes we may have achieved over the years: the academic and professional achievements, as well as the doors that have opened for promotion and access, especially if you come from humble beginnings, as many of us do. Many of us have surpassed the goals our parents set for us and are on our way to reaching even greater heights. Like Esther, who was the niece of an exile, orphaned, but chosen to vie for the position of queen amongst many other beautiful women, we have overcome many odds to get to where we are today and live our wildest dreams.

Now the king was attracted to Esther more than to any of the other women, and she won his favor and approval more than any of the other virgins. So he set a royal crown on her head and made her queen instead of Vashti. And the king gave a great banquet, Esther's banquet, for all his nobles and officials. He proclaimed a holiday throughout the provinces and distributed gifts with royal liberality. (Esther 2:17-18 – NIV).

As I sat in this story, I asked the Holy Spirit what He wanted me to share with you today, as we examine what appears to be a tale of triumph and great success. As He had me sit with the text for longer, a few things stood out that provided insight into my own journey, which I hope will do the same for you.

1. God orchestrated your entry.

That job, marriage, business, church, group of friends, or family could be a few of the areas you may have seen God divinely orchestrate success and growth. It is very easy to attribute success and growth to our own strength and effort, especially in a season where we are far from God. We cannot, however, forget that His plans for us are for good and to give us a hope and a future (see Jeremiah 29:11). Like Esther, your entry into that space of influence was pre-destined and carefully guided by God for a greater purpose.

2. Your gifts are a tool in God's hands.

Esther 2:17 says the King was more attracted to Esther than to any of the other women. Although commercialized and used by the world as a weapon against us, we see God's intentionality in the creation of woman: our natural design, the way our minds work, and the heart of nurturing and creativity are all tools that God placed within His daughters for influence. For Esther, we see that her beauty was a point of great favour, but it was her mind that eventually allowed her to beat her adversary—every gift, whether active or dormant, was intentionally placed within you.

You are a daughter of God; therefore, absolutely nothing about your life is a coincidence. No matter where you have found yourself today—signing documents in the boardroom, dropping off the kids at school, or turning the keys for your small business—you are a daughter of the King who is wooing you back to Him right where you are. I must remind you that your call and purpose are not confined to the four walls of a church, but that He has a purpose for you right where you are.

As you spend the time today going through your life, I ask you to stop and contemplate a few things:

- ***Your positioning is for kingdom purpose.***

"For if you remain silent at this time, relief and deliverance for the Jews will arise from another place, but you and your father's family will perish. And who knows but that you have come to your royal position for such a time as this?" (Esther 4:14 – NIV).

Though not revealed to Esther or even to Mordecai, a direct attack would come against the Jews of Xerxes's kingdom. God saw it beforehand and began to move strategically to place one of His daughters in a position of great influence as His secret weapon. **A time and a moment will come when God will put a demand on all He has placed within you as a daughter.**

- ***When the day of choice comes, choose God.***

Esther found herself in a very awkward position when Haman issued a decree against the Jews, her people. Her challenge was two-fold in nature. Firstly, she had not been summoned by the king in thirty days, and she was well aware of the rules that she could not, on her own, approach the king unless she had been summoned or the golden scepter had been extended. This meant Mordecai's request for her to plead mercy on the Jews' behalf meant risking sudden death. Esther had a tough choice to make, but she made the right one: she decided to stand as an advocate for her people against their enemy. Secondly, Esther was being asked to publicly step into an identity that had been hidden during all her preparation and reign as queen. No one knew she was a Jew, as that had been intentionally never shared, based on Mordecai's instruction. She was being asked to step out of that place where she was safely blending into her environment and reveal who she truly was. I believe many of us are like Esther; our secular identities have been armor that has kept us safe and out of the line of fire. However, when the time comes for us to choose, may we choose God.

- **Use kingdom tools to confront the enemy.**

for God gave us a spirit not of fear but of power and love and self-control. (2 Timothy 1:7 – ESV).

For the weapons of your warfare are not carnal, but are mighty through God for the pulling down of strongholds. (2 Corinthians 10:4 – NKJV).

You have been prepared for this, just like Esther, though it may seem daunting. You are equipped with a sound mind and knowledge on how to invoke heaven's backing in your situation. For Esther, once she had settled the storm in her own mind, she called a fast. Now known as the "Esther fast," this method was originally used by a queen in trouble who needed the backing of her heavenly King to face her earthy king. Esther drew on what she had been taught: enter no situation without prayer coverage; that as daughters, we win our battles, not with swords and spears, but through tactics downloaded from heaven. To be fair, reaching into a toolbox that you haven't used in a while or may not be familiar with can feel very awkward, but I am here to remind you today that you can do it. When faced with the crisis of an enemy confronting you, do not back down. Reclaim your position as daughter, dust off your tools, and fight!

ACTIVATION #4

With the help of the Holy Spirit, meditate on the following and answer the questions in your journal:

1. Identify a place of favour in your life where you credit the hand of God.

2. Do you know the purpose of your vocational calling?

3. By faith, write out a prayer for an issue you are facing in your workplace.

Where Are You?

Waiting On The Edge Of Promise

TODAY'S READING: GENESIS 18

In 2022, my friends and I decided to read the book "Crazy Faith" by Pastor Mike Todd, and to say we saw miracles while reading was an understatement. We saw breakthrough after breakthrough, miracle after miracle. Before we even started, I was excited. As the person who had gifted the friend group the book for Christmas, I was sure God was about to blow my mind. I had just applied for a big promotion, and my faith was at an all-time high. This was it! I was ready. As part of our reading of the book, we created a prayer plan; each person would have a dedicated day when everyone in the group would pray for them. I still remember it like yesterday. At about 5 am on the day the group was to pray for me, I received a message from my friend, Judisha: *"God said you are to read Psalm 37:34."*

With great expectation and half-open eyes, I scrambled to Google the verse. The very first word hit me like a ton of bricks: *"Wait."* I felt my heart sink. I don't think I even read the rest of the verse. I went back to bed.

I later sat in disappointment about what was to come. Despite doing my very best on that interview and actually scoring well, I did not get the job. The only thing I had was a promise: *"Wait for the LORD and keep his way, and he will exalt you to inherit the land; you will look on when the wicked are cut off." (Psalm 37:34 – ESV).*

My friend's timely delivery of that word would be the beginning of a long and trying season.

This leads us to a story about the matriarch of our faith, Sarah. We meet her first as Sarai in Genesis 11 as Abram's wife. We learn that she is beautiful but barren, which, in her culture, was a huge shame to carry.

We pick up her story in Genesis 15:2-4:

But Abram said, "O Lord GOD, what will you give me, for I continue childless, and the heir of my house is Eliezer of Damascus?" And Abram said, "Behold, you have given me no offspring, and a member of my household will be my heir." And behold, the word of the LORD came to him: "This man shall not be your heir; your very own son shall be your heir." (ESV).

Here we see God giving the promise to Abram that an heir would come. This promise was repeated in Genesis 17:15 and Genesis 18:10.

The place I would love us to spend some time in is Genesis 18:9-15, where Sarah responds to the promise:

Then they said to him, "Where is Sarah your wife?" And he said, "There, in the tent." He said, "I will surely return to you at this time next year; and behold, Sarah your wife will have a son." And Sarah was listening at the tent door, which was behind him. Now Abraham and Sarah were old, well advanced in years; she was past [the age of] childbearing. So Sarah laughed to herself [when she heard the LORD'S words], saying, "After I have become old, shall I have pleasure and delight, my lord (husband) being also old?" And the LORD *asked Abraham, "Why did Sarah laugh [to herself], saying, 'Shall I really give birth [to a child] when I am so old?' Is anything too difficult or too wonderful for the* LORD*? At the appointed time, when the season [for her delivery] comes, I will return to you and Sarah will have a son." Then Sarah denied it, saying, "I did not laugh"; because she was afraid. And He (the* LORD*) said, "No, but you did laugh." (AMP).*

There are two significant things to point out as we reflect on Sarah's story:

1. Her physical location was an indicator of her spiritual position.

From the story, we see that Sarah was standing outside the tent door, appearing to eavesdrop on the conversation between her husband and the three visitors. The Bible indicates that the visitor was the Lord and two angels. Sarah's position outside the tent may have been one intended for honor, but it is hard to overlook that it also reveals where she was. When the Lord outlines the promise that in a year from now, *Sarah will have a son,* we see Sarah standing outside the door and listening in on the conversation about her. For many of us, this is where we are: eavesdropping on the promises that God has for us, but never in the room. How many of us are at the door of a breakthrough but not in the place of intimacy where our promises are released?

2. Sarah's response revealed her heart.

Verse 12 shows us that Sarah laughed when she heard the promise, which prompted the verse that we heard quoted so often, *"Is anything too hard for God?"* Sarah's summation of the situation was that she was old, had been in menopause for a long time, and had a husband who was even older, so the promise, though good, was impossible. Her laughter is a strong indication of her own inner struggle of fear, doubt, and unbelief. Can you think of any promise from your own life that seemed impossible that you may have laughed just like Sarah? Is there something you want more than anything that God has given as a promise, but doubt—and even fear—has set in? For those who are unfamiliar with the story, Sarah's laugh was actually her second act of unbelief. In previous chapters, she had offered her servant, Hagar, to have a son on her behalf in her attempt to ensure the promise of God came to pass. Hagar was never God's plan for the promise, and so we see Ishmael being born, but unable to fulfill God's purpose.

In our journals, let's do a quick check of how similar we are to Sarah:

- Can we think of a promise that we may have received from God that remains unfulfilled?

- Can we identify any instance where we may have "helped" God and it backfired?

- Can we trace where unfulfilled promises may have affected our hearts toward God and even our walk with Him?

For me, the answer to all the questions above is a loud YES!

I recall receiving my first prophetic word at the age of 19 from Pastor Maggie Taylor of Agape Christian Fellowship. She said I would work with youth, get married, and everything would come in a package. As I write this book, seventeen years later, I have only seen a partial fulfillment of this promise. I believed that God would bless any man I chose, and so began a long string of poor relationship decisions. Over time, not only did I forget that promise, but also unbelief and fear took the place of faith. I no longer even believed that promise or had any expectation around it. For me, it may be marriage and family, but for you, it may be school, a business, healing, or a child. The Bible says, *"Hope deferred makes the heart sick, but a desire fulfilled is a tree of life."* (Proverbs 13:12 – ESV). Many of us have a relationship with God that has gone cold due to unfulfilled promises and desires. Our hearts have literally become sick, so when God reminds us of His promises for us, they die like the seed that fell on thorny soil.

As we close today, I hope to remind you that you are not alone. My own heart is still healing from promises that seem unfulfilled, and little by little, I am rebuilding my faith to hope again, to dream again, to wait with expectancy. I leave us with a few reminders from my own journey to hope:

1. Waiting is not punishment.

As I learnt through waiting for my promotion, the waiting period is necessary. It allowed me to grow as a person, which was eventually tested the day I signed on the dotted line for a higher-ranking position. It also taught me the character of God as a faithful God. It took two years for that promise to be fulfilled, and it was challenging. But I look back with gratitude at the work God did in me while I waited.

2. The story is not finished.

By faith even Sarah herself received the ability to conceive [a child], even [when she was long] past the normal age for it, because she considered Him who had given her the promise to be reliable and true [to His word]. (Hebrews 11:11 – AMP).

40

Despite her laugh, despite her unbelief, at some point Sarah re-engaged her faith one last time, and we finally see the birth of Isaac—the promised one. To top it off, Sarah was eventually recorded in the Faith Hall of Fame (see Hebrews 11:11).

This is a reminder that no matter where you are today, there is an opportunity to turn it around.

3. Protect your heart.

Proverbs 4:23 tells us to protect our hearts, for from it flow the issues of life. When the Bible speaks of the heart, it does not refer to our physical organ, but rather uses the word to convey the totality of our inner being. We are governed from this one point of unity. Disappointment and even a prolonged season of waiting can have a deep impact on our hearts. Building a deeper relationship with God and the Word, serving others, and fanning the flames of hope and faith are a few ways to protect our hearts as we wait.

ACTIVATION #5

1. Ask the Holy Spirit to show you a promise you may have given up on and why.

2. Pray for God to reveal His Word concerning this promise.

3. Share with a close friend your experience with waiting on this promise and ask for prayer.

WEEK 2

THE FATHER'S HEART

My frame was not hidden from You, when I was being formed in secret, and intricately and skillfully formed [as if embroidered with many colors] in the depths of the earth. Your eyes have seen my unformed substance; And in Your book were all written the days that were appointed for me, when as yet there was not one of them [even taking shape]. How precious also are Your thoughts to me, O God! How vast is the sum of them! If I could count them, they would outnumber the sand. When I awake, I am still with You. (Psalm 139:15-18 – AMP).

This week, we will spend time exploring the love of the Father in its most tangible ways. Stories will range from the woman at the well to the Daughters of Zelophedad. Though we are taught that God loves us, we must be open to experiencing it. As we go through this week, may you be reminded that you were beautifully formed and intimately known. His thoughts for you are precious; how vast is the sum of them (see Psalm 139:17). May we never forget that we serve a God who will not only go out of His way for us but will sacrifice His own Son to restore His relationship with us.

May you be reminded of this radical love for you this week!

Let's go!

The Father's Heart:

I Love You

TODAY'S READING: JOHN 3:16

Every Good Friday, my church does what they call a prayer line. This is where all the pastors form a line like a guard of honor and pray for each person as they pass through the line. I still remember it, even though this was over four years ago, because I had never seen it before. As I entered the line, one of the female pastors placed her hands on my chest and said, *"God heal this broken heart, heal this broken heart. I cover you in God's love."* As she continued to pray, the dam within me broke.

In full transparency, the most challenging part of restoring my relationship with God was accepting God's love. It took months—years—to accept that God's love was freely given and nothing could truly separate me from His love. It was hard for me to accept, and it may be the same for you. With that in mind, we are examining a foundational principle of our faith: love.

For God so loved the world, that he gave his only begotten Son, that whosoever believeth in him should not perish, but have everlasting life. For God sent not his Son into the world to condemn the world; but that the world through him might be saved. (John 3:16-17 – KJV).

BREAKDOWN OF LOVE

Above, we have a verse that we learnt as children, one that many can still recite from memory. However, how many of us have ever truly understood the meaning of this verse? I still remember watching The Passion of the Christ for the very first time and whispering to God, *"You should not have done it. We weren't worth the sacrifice of Jesus."* The truth is, we are not. However, when we examine what love truly is, we see that God the Father embodies the ultimate definition of love, which is selfless sacrifice. Let's look at a scripture that is read at weddings and preached on Valentine's Day: 1 Corinthians 13:4-7:

Love is patient, love is kind. It does not envy, it does not boast, it is not proud. It does not dishonor others, it is not self-seeking, it is not easily angered, it keeps no record of wrongs. Love does not delight in evil but rejoices with the truth. It always protects, always trusts, always hopes, always perseveres. (NIV).

As we start this week, we must build on this fundamental truth: God loves you! Let me say it again: God loves you! Yes, you with the broken heart, the guilt, the shame, the one who walked away. Yes, you. This week, we will be spending our time looking at the heart of the Father and its varying attributes, and how they have shown up in the Bible, and hopefully, will become real in our lives.

Unless we can truly accept that we are loved—truly loved—we will struggle in this journey of restoration. It is His love that pulls us back to Him, that draws us back into deep intimacy with Him as He waits with outstretched hands. Despite our mental understanding of His love for us, many of us have found ourselves in a place where we can no longer experience His love.

But how do we get to that place where the love of Father is something we cannot openly receive? Let us look at one way we are drawn away from the Father's love: the Book of James clues us into what may have happened: *"Temptation comes from our own desires, which entice us and drag us away." (James 1:14 - NLT).*

Is there anything that has enticed you? Has it dragged you away?

Eve was enticed through her ear and eye and ate from the forbidden tree.
David was enticed through his eye and had sex with Bathsheba.
Judas was enticed by money and betrayed Jesus.
Jodianna was enticed by her need for companionship and backslid from her faith.

_____was enticed by_____ and _____ (fill in the blank).

As you reflect to fill in the blank, one thing is true: both Eve and David lived to experience the redemptive love of God, with David even being called a man after God's own heart (see 1 Samuel 13:14).

We have all these great examples of people who encountered the love of the Father, were enticed, fell away, and were restored, so why not us?

What causes this chasm that prevents us from receiving a gift freely given, even if we have messed up?

The reasons are many, but today I will take a deeper dive into two of the many reasons that I hope you can identify with and call out, if they are lurking in your experience of God, the Father.

ACCEPTANCE BY WORKS

Due to our culture and various standards of performance, the idea that we serve a God who promises to be with us, even if we make our bed in hell, is hard to imagine. I struggled with the concept of love by works. For years, I carried a belief that my mistakes—my sin—made me harder to love. I believed that God's love for me had limits, and my mind could not wrap around a God who loved me, even in my mistakes. You see, our sin is why Jesus came. If we were perfect, we would not need the sacrifice of Jesus. While this does not give us permission to trample this gift underfoot, it is a gift freely given. It is for our mess that Jesus died; the very voice of accusation that has kept us stuck was silenced on the cross by the ultimate gift of love. Love by works is also something we could have learnt from our homes, where our worth was validated by grades or good behavior. We were celebrated for good and ostracized when we missed the mark.

FORGIVENESS

The second hindrance to our accepting the free gift of love is a big F-word. Yes! But not in the way we are expecting. While for many of us, the inability to forgive the abuse, the offense, the lie has hindered us from accepting the love of God, there are two other layers of forgiveness I want to highlight:

1. **Forgiveness of God**: Yes, I said it. While it is very rarely said, if we were to turn the searchlight on our hearts, we may find that hidden beneath the numbness of our hearts is a slight accusation levied at God. For years, I harbored a very subtle resentment that God was God and therefore I could have been married or promoted by now. I know He is all-

powerful, and He was not doing it for me. Years of that built up an iron wall.

2. **Forgiveness of self**: I remember being at the altar while Yvonne looked me in the eye and said, *"God has forgiven you. Now you need to forgive yourself."* It felt like she had stung me, and I staggered backward. I had never heard that before. I left the altar that day feeling more confused than when I went for prayer. I soon learned that forgiving ourselves is a major part of our restoration, as well as openly accepting the Father's love. For many of us, the results of our actions have led to shame and guilt, which have hidden the need for us not only to accept the gift of forgiveness given but also to take the hard step of forgiving ourselves.

As we close, I encourage us to spend some time in Romans 8, and I pray we will have a mighty encounter with the overwhelming love of the Father:

What then shall we say to all these things? If God is for us, who can be [successful] against us? He who did not spare [even] His own Son, but gave Him up for us all, how will He not also, along with Him, graciously give us all things? Who will bring any charge against God's elect (His chosen ones)? It is God who justifies us [declaring us blameless and putting us in a right relationship with Himself]. Who is the one who condemns us? Christ Jesus is the One who died [to pay our penalty], and more than that, who was raised [from the dead], and who is at the right hand of God interceding [with the Father] for us. Who shall ever separate us from the love of Christ? Will tribulation, or distress, or persecution, or famine, or nakedness, or danger, or sword? (Romans 8:31-35 – AMP).

Jesus loves you. Period.

ACTIVATION #1

With the Holy Spirit, reflect on the following:

1. What part of the definition of love seems the most difficult to apply to your life now?

2. Is there any area of forgiveness you can identify that may be stopping you from experiencing the love of God?

3. Are you ready to experience the baptism of God's love? (Ask Him).

The Father's Heart:

I See You

TODAY'S READING: GENESIS 16:7-13

Rejected. Pregnant. Running—a few of the words that could be used to describe the situation Hagar was in as she fled the harsh treatment of her mistress, Sarai, the wife of Abraham. Just months before, Hagar was seen as a solution to a promise God had made. God had promised Abram a seed, and Sarah, his wife, was barren. Sarah devised a plan. Her slave, Hagar, would bear the promised child, and she did. However, in the blink of an eye, Hagar went from a solution to an actual problem to be dealt with. Hagar's newfound importance caused friction between the women, and Hagar decided to run.

Today, we pick up with our exploration of the Father's heart with a woman on the run; a woman facing rejection from her masters.

The angel of the LORD found her by a spring of water in the wilderness, the spring on the way to Shur. And he said, "Hagar, servant of Sarai, where have you come from and where are you going?" She said, "I am fleeing from my mistress Sarai." The angel of the LORD said to her, "Return to your mistress and submit to her." The angel of the LORD also said to her, "I will surely multiply your offspring so that they cannot be numbered for multitude." And the angel of the LORD said to her, "Behold, you are pregnant and shall bear a son. You shall call his name Ishmael, because the LORD has listened to your affliction. He shall be a wild donkey of a man, his hand against everyone and everyone's hand against him, and he shall dwell over against all his kinsmen." So she called the name of the LORD who spoke to her, "You are a God of seeing," for she said, "Truly here I have seen him who looks after me." Therefore the well was called Beer-lahai-roi; it lies between Kadesh and Bered. (Genesis 16:7-14 - ESV).

In the story of Hagar, we are introduced to a key element of God's character, the God who sees—Jehovah Roi. Hagar, on the run from her mistress, rejected from where she would have served, was so moved by her encounter that she named God "Roi," which means *"I have seen the One who sees me."* This is recorded as the first instance where God is named, giving us insight into the deep complexity of the God we serve. I want us to zoom in and notice who had this encounter: a pregnant Egyptian slave on the run from the wrath of her owner. It was she to whom God revealed this dimension of Himself to.

Hagar's naming of God reveals how she felt about her encounter with God. Hagar felt seen. She could have named Him the God who gives promises or the God who finds the slave in the wilderness, but she named Him "El Roi" as He touched her at her greatest point of need: where her wound was. God saw her!

In a world where we are constantly connected to the world but far from deep, meaningful interactions, it is critical that we explore this theme of being seen. Psychology Today described the need to be seen as a basic need for all humans. We need to be seen by our family, our friends, and we need to be seen in the world at large. Today, I pose the question: Do you feel seen? Yes or no? In some areas more than others?

No matter your answer, I want to introduce or reintroduce you to someone.

You are madly loved and being pursued by the God who sees!

It was Him whom Hagar met in the wilderness as she was making her way back home, escaping from her mistress. From this short encounter, we learn a few lessons about the heart of the Father:

1. His eyes are on you.

Genesis 16:7 says, *"The angel of the LORD found her by a spring of water in the wilderness, the spring on the way to Shur." (ESV)*. It says God "found" her. That word inherently implies intent, as if she were being searched for. No matter where you are today, God's heart beats for you, and He is pulling you home. For some of us, even now, we feel the gentle tug of God on our hearts in so many unique ways. We see Him show up for us in various life circumstances. His eyes are on you. Like the true heart of a Father, He seeks to protect and bless us. Nothing you do can change that. His love for you knows no bounds, and He will find you.

2. He will invite you to take action.

The angel not only showed up for encouragement but also gave Hagar some very specific instructions.

The angel of the LORD said to her, "Return to your mistress and submit to her." (Genesis 16:9 - ESV).

When I read this, I had to do a double-take. Why would God send her back to the place of pain that she was escaping from? Sometimes God sends us back to the place to confront it or to extract the treasures He has hidden just for us. Though not all of us will be nudged to go back, what is the instruction you are sensing today?

3. He has a promise for you, no matter the circumstance.

We see God releasing a promise over her son's life, which gave Hagar the fuel to go back under Sarai's rule. It was that promise that gave her hope to go through all the many things that would eventually face her, including having to leave with her teenage son years later. God saw Hagar in a culture and a circumstance where she was not expecting to be seen or even heard. Pregnant, alone, in a wilderness, yet God revealed Himself to a slave girl running from her mistress, and she named Him, *"I have seen the One who sees me."*

GOD AS EL ROI

Though mentioned only once in the scriptures as El Roi, it is an attribute of God the Father that has a special place in my heart. I encountered Him as El Roi in a season when I felt invisible and fading into the background. As shared on one of the previous days, twice in 2023, God sent a word to me through two separate women of God to come out of the shadows. To be honest, I had retreated from life in many ways and had become extremely comfortable living in the shadows, in the background, rarely seen and definitely not heard. Yet, He sent not one but two of His daughters to let me know, *"I see you!"*

He saw me hiding in the shadows, on the edge of promise but not quite stepping into the light. I encountered El Roi, who saw me even when I didn't see myself and didn't know quite where I was. Today, I introduce you to El Roi, the one who sees young women on the run from their past but not quite on their way to destiny—

women who seem to have it all but are feeling a little lost inside. Today, I introduce you to the God who caught all your tears in a bottle and knows the number of hairs on your head.

You may ask why?

The answer is simple: as a daughter of God, what you are carrying is too important, and you are too important to Him.

ACTIVATION #2

For our activation today, I pose the questions that were posed to Hagar:

1. Where have you come from?

2. Where are you going?

3. What areas would you love God to reveal His promises to you?

Amidst the noise and the chaos, may the longing of your heart be met; to be fully seen and fully loved.

The Father's Heart:

I Hear Your Petition

TODAY'S READING: NUMBERS 27:1-4

As we continue on the beautiful journey of discovering the Father's love for you—His daughter—we will spend some time with five sisters mentioned over five times in the Bible, but were not widely taught to us growing up. Today, we meet the daughters of Zelophehad: Mahlah, Noah, Hoglah, Milcah, and Tirzah. We find their very impactful story in Numbers 27.

Then drew near the daughters of Zelophehad the son of Hepher, son of Gilead, son of Machir, son of Manasseh, from the clans of Manasseh the son of Joseph. The names of his daughters were: Mahlah, Noah, Hoglah, Milcah, and Tirzah. And they stood before Moses and before Eleazar the priest and before the chiefs and all the congregation, at the entrance of the tent of meeting, saying, "Our father died in the wilderness. He was not among the company of those who gathered themselves together against the Lord in the company of Korah, but died for his own sin. And he had no sons. Why should the name of our father be taken away from his clan because he had no son? Give to us a possession among our father's brothers." (Numbers 27:1-4 – ESV).

Let us add some context here. According to the law that governed the Israelites, when a man died, his possessions were to go to his sons, and if no sons, they passed to his brothers. It was expected that daughters would marry and be taken care of by the tribe into which they married, but here we had a unique situation: a set of sisters whose father had died, but there were no sons, and none of them had yet married. They stood to lose their inheritance as well as their means of surviving.

They did something unthinkable. They did something bold. They took their inheritance, their father's legacy, and their survival into their own hands and approached the men whom God had put in place to lead and oversee the law. They put their case before Moses, and Moses took their case to God.

It is here that we see a dimension of the heart of the Father that made me pause. You see, we all have a perception of how God is, especially God the Father. For me, I saw the Godhead like this: God, the Father: Firm, strict, unmoving; God, the Son (Jesus): Warm, inviting, forgiving, and gracious and God, the Holy Spirit: a guide and constantly with me.

Now, I know there are many differing beliefs around God, but what I want to challenge us on are these three questions:

- How do we see God?

- What is the persona that we have attached to Him?

- How does it affect how we receive from Him?

It's important to challenge those thoughts as they are limiting how we are experiencing God.

THE HEART OF THE FATHER

Moses brought their case before the Lord. And the Lord said to Moses, "The daughters of Zelophehad are right. You shall give them possession of an inheritance among their father's brothers and transfer the inheritance of their father to them." (Numbers 27:5-7 – ESV).

Here we see a few characteristics of the heart of the Father in this text. Let's explore:

1. He listens and cares.

The first thing we see God saying to Moses is that the daughters of Zelophehad are right. God agreed with their case, despite it being a decades-old law that excluded daughters from an inheritance. God heard the case and ruled in their Favor. Today, I want to take the opportunity to remind you that God cares and He listens. The act of these five sisters is a vivid example of *Hebrews 4:16: "Let us have confidence, then, and approach God's throne, where there is grace. There we will receive mercy and find grace to help us just when we need it." (GNT).* We have an open invitation to bring our case before God.

2. He judges fairly.

In reading this story, it could have gone many ways. Moses could have not presented their case to maintain the status quo, or God could have said no, but He listened to their case and ruled fairly. This dimension of God is something we often forget when we have gone our own way and our hearts have gone cold. Not only did God rule on their behalf favourably, but He set a precedent for unmarried daughters. In a world that can still be unkind to the widowed, the barren, the unmarried, or even the perceived unsuccessful, we see God making provision for these five sisters and all who would follow after them.

3. He is a God of legacy.

We see in Joshua 17 the actual apportioning of the land after the Israelites entered the promised land. The daughters reminded Joshua, who had succeeded Moses, of what God had said and claimed their inheritance. Today, I want to remind you that God cares about your legacy, the legacy you will leave for your children. He wants you to prosper as your soul prospers, and that includes your children and your children's children.

LET US REASON TOGETHER

The opening Chapter of Isaiah is where I want to leave you today. Isaiah 1:18 says, *"Come now, let us reason together, says the Lord: though your sins are like scarlet, they shall be as white as snow; though they are red like crimson, they shall become like wool." (ESV)*. We have learned today that we have a God who listens and invites us to come to him and talk. The truth is, God can handle our anger, our cares, our disappointments, and the injustices that we have endured. Today, He is inviting you to come and reason. He is ready to listen.

ACTIVATION #3

1. Is there a case you need to take before God?

2. Write the case in prayer format with a date in your journal.

The Father's Heart:

Zoe Life

TODAY'S READING: JOHN 10:10

Today, our exploration of the heart of the Father will take us into various stories found in the New Testament that carry a common theme: bringing dead things to life. That will be the topic of our exploration today: Life and life more abundantly.

The thief comes only in order to steal and kill and destroy. I came that they may have and enjoy life, and have it in abundance [to the full, till it overflows]. (John 10:10 – AMP).

Now, when looking at the meaning of abundant life, there can be many interpretations as to what this means for the daughter of God. This interpretation may range from financial wealth to an ability to enjoy the simple blessings of God both here and in the life to come. Before we go any further today, I want you to define what an abundant life means to you.

For me, an abundant life means *health and wealth, while living on purpose and in purpose.*

What does it mean for you?

No matter what your definition of an abundant life is, the scripture has clearly stated that it is God's wish for you, His daughter. We cannot, however, overlook the first part of John 10:10 that points out a real threat to this promise of God. The thief comes to steal, kill, and destroy. No matter where you are in your walk with God today, I need you to know this. You have a real enemy, and his purpose is clear: to steal your joy, peace, and purpose, to kill your dreams and passion for God and others, and to ultimately destroy you and your legacy.

Accepting that as a daughter of God, I had a real enemy but a defeated one was a pivotal point in my walk. Against this backdrop of God's desire for every one of His daughters to have an abundant life, we will walk along with Jesus as He did three of His most noteworthy miracles: raising people from the dead.

Soon afterward Jesus went to a city called Nain [near Nazareth], and His disciples and a large crowd accompanied Him. Now as He approached the city gate, a dead man was being carried out—the only son of his mother, and she was a widow. And a large crowd from the city was with her [in the funeral procession]. When the Lord saw her, He felt [great] compassion for her, and said to her, "Do not weep." And He came up and touched the bier [on which the body rested], and the pallbearers stood still. And He said, "Young man, I say to you, arise [from death]!" The man who was dead sat up and began to speak. And Jesus gave him back to his mother. (Luke 7:11-15 – AMP).

Then a woman who had suffered from a hemorrhage for twelve years came up behind Him and touched the [tassel] fringe of His outer robe; for she had been saying to herself, "If I only touch His outer robe, I will be healed." But Jesus turning and seeing her said, "Take courage, daughter; your [personal trust and confident] faith [in Me] has made you well." And at once the woman was [completely] healed. When Jesus came to the ruler's house, and saw the flute players [who were professional, hired mourners] and the [grieving] crowd

making an uproar, He said, "Go away; for the girl is not dead, but is sleeping."
And they laughed and jeered at Him. But when the crowd had been sent outside,
Jesus went in and took her by the hand, and the girl got up. (Matthew 9:20–
25 – AMP).

Jesus, once more deeply moved, came to the tomb. It was a cave with a stone laid
across the entrance. "Take away the stone," he said. "But, Lord," said Martha,
the sister of the dead man, "by this time there is a bad odor, for he has been
there four days." Then Jesus said, "Did I not tell you that if you believe, you
will see the glory of God?" So they took away the stone. Then Jesus looked up
and said, "Father, I thank you that you have heard me. I knew that you always
hear me, but I said this for the benefit of the people standing here, that they may
believe that you sent me." When he had said this, Jesus called in a loud voice,
"Lazarus, come out!" The dead man came out, his hands and feet wrapped
with strips of linen, and a cloth around his face. Jesus said to them, "Take off
the grave clothes and let him go." (John 11:38- 44 – NIV).

Within the beautiful layers of these stories, we learn a lot about the
heart of the Father as reflected through His Son, Jesus.

1. He has the power to revive dead things.

At the tomb of Lazarus, Jesus reveals a dimension of Himself that
Martha was about to experience.

Jesus said to her, "I am the resurrection and the life. Whoever believes in me, though
he die, yet shall he live. (John 11:25 - ESV).

Inherent in who Jesus was as God was the power to resurrect and
bring dead things to life. We see Him being moved to raise three
different persons from the dead during His ministry. Today, let us
ponder our own lives and highlight any areas that may be dead, any
areas where we are not seeing the abundant life that God has
promised us as His daughters. Are they dead and buried like

Lazarus was, or being carried out on a stretcher by your own doubt and fear? You serve a God who specializes in raising dead things.

2. His Word has power.

In each of these accounts, we realize that Jesus used a pattern I would love for us to look at in some detail. To Lazarus, He gave an instruction, *"Lazarus, come out."* To the son of the widow of Nain, He said, *"Young man, I say to you, arise [from death]!"* We have other instances, for example, when Jesus healed the paralytic, he instructed him, *"Get up, pick up your stretcher and go home."* I am taking the time to highlight that the words your Father uses have within them the creative power to bring dead things to life.

What words have you been given about that dream that seems to have died, or where you have given up hope? Today, I remind you that His life-giving words have the power to bring dead things to life. Like the prophet Ezekiel, I urge you today as a daughter of God to use the Word to call all dead things back to life.

3. Your family matters to God.

The third point I would like to take the time to mention is that God cares not only about you but also about your family. In all three instances, we realize that we meet a family member of the person who died. He was moved by the family member. We meet Jairus in his role as a father, the widow of Nain as a mother, and Mary and Martha as sisters. For most of us, our families are some of our greatest concerns, and today, I want to remind you that God will move with compassion by the pain you feel over your family. He cares about the marriage, children, parents, and wider family group. When God saw the pain of a mother burying her son, He moved. When He saw the pain of a father losing his daughter, He moved.

God is ready to move on your family's behalf and speak life into all dead situations.

So, as we close for today, I bring our attention back to the verse that we started the day with: *"The thief comes only in order to steal and kill and destroy. I came that they may have and enjoy life, and have it in abundance [to the full, till it overflows]." (John 10:10 – AMP).*

I want to remind you today, as a daughter of God, no matter the situation or how far you may feel, you serve a God who can restore what has been stolen, killed, or destroyed. He has proven Himself to be a restorer and is ready to do the same for you.

ACTIVATION #4

1. What areas of your life have you seen the work of the enemy (steal, kill, or destroy)?

2. Is there a family member or situation that you would love to bring before Jesus?

3. Write one dream or desire you would love God to bring back to life?

The Father's Heart:

I Will Go Out Of My Way For You

TODAY'S READING: JOHN 4

I can recall many instances when I walked into a church service unaware that it was the day when God's presence would arrest me fully. Our story today takes us to an interesting encounter with a Samaritan woman.

In John 4, we find her going about her daily routine of drawing water at midday when she would be alone and have the well all to herself. What she did not bargain for was that this day would be the day her life would change completely.

Then a woman from Samaria came to draw water. Jesus said to her, "Give Me a drink"— For His disciples had gone off into the city to buy food—The Samaritan woman asked Him, "How is it that You, being a Jew, ask me, a Samaritan woman, for a drink?" (For Jews have nothing to do with Samaritans.) Jesus answered her, "If you knew [about] God's gift [of eternal life], and who it is who says, 'Give Me a drink,' you would have asked Him [instead], and He would have given you living water (eternal life)." (John 4:7-10 – AMP).

This popular and well-known story is a beautiful illustration of the Father's heart. It provides key insights into how God is intentional about seeking us out. Let us examine what we learn from this story.

— Jesus Showed Up In Her Routine Of Isolation

We meet the Samaritan woman drawing water in the midday sun; it was not the typical time for the women to gather at the well. Her routine was outside the norm; however, Jesus was able to find her within her routine of isolation. The Bible says He was sitting at the well after He had sent His disciples off. Her encounter with Jesus needed to be personal and intentional, and she found Him waiting for her. This story vividly reveals that God's heart is not limited to the four walls of the church, and His pursuit of you—His daughter—is intentional. He will find you, whether through a dream, a colleague at work, a song, or just about anything. His heart for you is a life-changing encounter with Him.

— He Met Her at a Point of Need: Thirst

Water is described as the source of life, with our bodies being made up of 50-75% water, and the earth being 71% water. Water is a need for all of us, and the Samaritan woman was no different. In the text, we meet her satisfying a basic human need, but her needs were much greater, and Jesus pointed to them in his conversation with her. He realized that there was something driving her: a thirst for something that was not being satisfied.

In John 4:16, Jesus asked her to go call her husband and come back; she responds by sharing she has none. Jesus then reveals her condition to her, but not without hope. She had previously had five husbands and was now with someone who was not her husband. It is clear that she was searching for something that none of her husbands could fulfill. She was being driven by a thirst that her culture, isolation, or relationships could not meet. The Father's heart in this story went straight to the point of need: her thirst.

65

— He Used Her Knowledge to Move Her Into Revelation

The woman at the well demonstrates a powerful journey that we all go through in our spiritual journey. I term it the knowledge to revelation shift, which occurs when a piece of information (knowledge) becomes living and breathing within us and causes change. The Samaritan woman shows two points of knowledge in her conversation:

1. *"Sir,"* the woman said, *"I can see that you are a prophet."* (see John 4:19).

2. The woman said, *"I know that Messiah (called Christ) is coming. When he comes, he will explain everything to us."* (see John 4:25).

In John 4:26, Jesus confirms her knowledge and reveals Himself to her: *"I am He!"*

What we see next is a life that has walked into the revelation of who Jesus is. Her knowledge was now revelation and was standing right in front of her. She left the jar—her means of survival—and went to the very people she was in isolation from, and was hailed one of the first evangelists in the Bible. Her meeting with the Messiah prompted a response in her that changed her life.

Then, leaving her water jar, the woman went back to the town and said to the people, "Come, see a man who told me everything I ever did. Could this be the Messiah?" They came out of the town and made their way toward him. (John 4:28-30 – NIV).

This story is one of many that shows that the heart of the Father is one that pursues us and chases after us with intentionality. The greatest display of this is shared in one of the most well-known verses in the Bible: John 3:16: *"For God so loved the world, that he gave his only Son, that whoever believes in him should not perish but have eternal life." (ESV)*.

To separate from one's only son has to be one of the most painful experiences for a father to go through. Yet we see Jesus take on human form and subject Himself to the rules and limitations of human flesh to be able to pay the ultimate penalty for our sin. When Jesus was on the cross (as depicted in several movies) and cried out, *"Father, why have You forsaken me?"*, my heart always breaks as He was facing total disconnection with His Father. But why? For us! His willingness to go out of His way was not limited to going through Samaria but was encapsulated by His ultimate death for us, His daughters.

We close with a reminder from Psalm 139:8: *"If I ascend to heaven, you are there; if I make my bed in Sheol (the nether world, the place of the dead), behold, You are there." (AMP, emphasis mine)*. I want to remind you that you are on His mind and He will find you in good and bad places. Today, my prayer is that He would find you wherever you are.

ACTIVATION #5

1. Have you ever felt unreachable by God?

2. Where is a place you believe God could not reach you?

WEEK 3

JOURNEY TO THE FATHER

I will arise and go to my father, and I will say to him, "Father, I have sinned against heaven and before you. I am no longer worthy to be called your son. Treat me as one of your hired servants."' And he arose and came to his father. But while he was still a long way off, his father saw him and felt compassion, and ran and embraced him and kissed him. (Luke 15:18-20 - ESV).

We often hear that every journey begins with a step. My prayer is that by now, your heart has been softened, your walls are down, and your experience with the love of God has been renewed.

It is time to take action.

Each of the days ahead is focused on making one step closer towards our journey of restoration, but it starts with the first move. The gift of restoration is promised to every daughter of God.

Will You Take It?

This week, my heart for you is to take your time and meditate on the call to action that each day brings.

PS: If you made it to this section, I am extremely proud of you and grateful for your healing and restoration! For the last time until we meet again, Let's Go!

Journey To The Father:

Know The Seasons

TODAY'S READING: ECCLESIASTES 3:1

Summer. Winter. Spring. Autumn. Yes! You guessed it. Today, we will spend our time together looking at seasons and understanding our seasons.

Seasons are all around us. As women, we have a monthly cycle, as well as seasons of childhood, puberty, reproductive years, and menopause. In our spiritual life, it is no different.

Can you identify your spiritual season?

— **Summer:** Seasons of joy and gladness: God's blessing, bounty, and fruitfulness to steward and water.

— **Fall:** A season of harvest and reaping.

— **Winter:** A season of isolation and hibernation, deep reflection, where faith is strengthened and foundations solidified.

— **Spring:** A season of new blooms, fresh revelation, and taking action.

You may be wondering how knowing your spiritual season qualifies as an active step in restoring your relationship with your heavenly Father. I propose that it forms the foundation for our entire week.

Today, we open in 1 Chronicles 12:32, *"from Issachar, men who understood the times and knew what Israel should do—200 chiefs, with all their relatives under their command." (NIV).*

This verse opens our eyes to a powerful revelation that there were people who not only understood the times but also knew what Israel should do. Having an understanding of where I am is also an indicator of what I should do on my spiritual journey. Even as I write this book, I am on the brink of exiting a wilderness season spiritually. I was once a vibrant, young youth leader on fire for God who also danced on the worship team. I faded into the wintery background of isolation and hibernation. If I am honest with you, I became comfortable in this season until God began to plant seeds of reconciliation and hope, signaling that He was initiating a new season.

Again, I pose the question to you: *What season are you in?*

I was made fully aware of the season I was in by words that were prayed over me, which I shared with you before in *"Come out of the shadows."* In my own eyes, I felt fine. I had devotion occasionally, listened to sermons, and popped into church. I was even being blessed financially and in my career. But there was no fire, no passion, and honestly, no interest, but those words planted an awareness of my situation in me that I couldn't shake. For me, God used someone else to plant that deep awareness.

Can you identify when your own spiritual season shifted and what may have prompted it? Was it a dream, a call from an old mentor, or a crisis? Though the ways are many, one thing we can be certain of is that once God has marked you for purpose, His love will always chase after you. Let us look at some of our sisters in the Bible who received a divine call from God and how it changed their season.

Through your job and a national crisis.

Deborah, the only female judge in Israel, made a decision to go to war based on the oppression that her people were going through, and at the special request of Barak to join him (see Judges 4)—after twenty years of oppression, the time for a change of season had come. Could God be using the state of your nation, your community, your family to get your attention and drive you to deeper intimacy with Him?

Through a mentor.

In the book of Ruth, we see Naomi, the mother-in-law, guiding her on how to use cultural practices to make her interest in Boaz known. Often, our mentors or leaders will be the ones God uses to nudge us and get our attention to the season we are in and the urgency to address it.

Through an encounter.

We head over to the New Testament, where Jesus encounters Mary Magdalene, who was possessed by seven demons, and He freed her. She then became a part of His ministry here on earth. An encounter with Jesus marked her season of change and purpose. I can personally relate to a deep encounter with God's presence being the trigger point for a new season.

Though in no way exhaustive, I took the time to share those instances as they remind us of how dynamic God is and that He will use various means to get through to us.

As we close today, I leave us with this nugget from John 6:44, *"No one is able to come to Me unless the Father Who sent Me attracts and draws him and gives him the desire to come to Me." (AMPC)*. In this season, no matter where you are, your heavenly Father is drawing you to Himself to recommitment, intimacy, and a deeper, richer spiritual life. John 6 lets us know that we are unable to come to Him of our own will and must be drawn by Him. Being sought, loved, and chosen by the God of the universe is a privilege and an honor for each of us. I leave us with this: *"Today, if you hear his voice, do not harden your hearts as in the rebellion." (Hebrews 3:15 – ESV)*. It is very easy for the noise of our lives and the pain of our past to crowd out the gentle nudge of God, but I invite us not to harden our hearts through rejecting God or becoming insensitive to His conviction of sin.

ACTIVATION #1

1. Can you clearly identify which season you are in spiritually?

2. Do you feel God drawing you today, and how will you respond?

Journey to the Father:

It Takes A Decision

TODAY'S READING: LUKE 15:13-21

Home. That word means different things for different people, but for me, it has only good memories. "Home" for me is the long drive up a winding terrain to the cool, cool hills of Alexandria, St. Ann. It is still, to this day, one of my favorite things to do, and just thinking about it triggers memories of loud chaotic laughter, my father's mannish water on a Saturday morning and my mother's strict boundaries that kept the family together. While I am aware that not everyone has warm, fuzzy memories when they think of home, we will be spending our time examining a story of a son who made his way back home and take from him lessons we can apply to our journey.

Then He said, "A certain man had two sons. The younger of them [inappropriately] said to his father, 'Father, give me the share of the property that falls to me.' So he divided the estate between them. A few days later, the younger son gathered together everything [that he had] and traveled to a distant country, and there he wasted his fortune in reckless and immoral living. Now when he had spent everything, a severe famine occurred in that country, and he began to do without and be in need. So he went and forced himself on one of the citizens of that country, who sent him into his fields to feed pigs. He would have gladly eaten the [carob] pods that the pigs were eating [but they could not satisfy his hunger], and no one was giving anything to him. But

75

when he [finally] came to his senses, he said, 'How many of my father's hired men have more than enough food, while I am dying here of hunger! (Luke 15:11-16 – AMP).

This very popular story outlines the journey of a son who has claimed his inheritance and left home. The Bible describes that he quickly spent all he had and had to feed swine because of his quick and painful fall from grace. Most of our time will be spent in the middle of the story, which is the foundation of the final section of this book.

HE CAME TO HIS SENSES

Luke 15:17 is a verse that has long plagued me on my own journey, *"and he came to his senses." (NASB).*

The process of coming to one's senses can be painful and, in many cases, a regretful one, as it inherently implies that one was acting outside of what is known to be true and outside of the realm of good sense. When we look at the passage, we see three triggers that may have influenced the prodigal son's moment of introspection.

1. **There was severe famine in the land.**

Our external circumstances often act as a catalyst for change. When we look around our external world, we see wars, heightened petrol and food prices, and racism, which are just a few of the circumstances that make the world around us feel unsafe. The prodigal son, like us, was not immune to the external factors that could affect him.

2. He was hungry and had nothing to eat.

Not only was his external world in a state of famine, but his immediate circumstances were also deteriorating. The Bible tells us his money had run out, and he was hungry. The feeling of true hunger may be a feeling many of us are not acquainted with, but food, water, and air are necessary for life. When the Bible takes the time to describe that he was craving the food that the pigs were eating, we become fully aware of how desperate his situation had become.

3. He remembered the love and care of his father.

Contrasted against the background of enjoying his money and spending everything he had, he remembered home. The love of his father, the access he had, and the life he used to live. Aware that his actions have revoked that access, he turns his mind to the servants in his father's house, who also were taken care of and had enough food to spare while he was starving.

Can you identify anything currently in your life that is driving you back home to the Father? For the purpose of this book, home is the place of relationship between you and God, where your communion is not broken.

Are we ready to come to our senses?

THE POWER OF REPENTANCE AND HUMILITY

The story of the prodigal son is powerful in that it gives us a front row seat into the internal dialogue happening in the mind of the son as he prepares to return home. It is here we realize that "coming to our senses" is not only a mental process but a process of the heart. We continue in Luke 15:18-19, which gives us two critical elements needed when we are rebuilding our relationship with God, and generally to maintain our relationship with Him.

1. Repentance

"I have sinned against you and against heaven, I am no longer worthy to be called your son."

There comes a point in our journey, whether we are backsliders, lukewarm, or simply not yet saved, where, like the prodigal son, we must acknowledge our actions and the consequences they bring. If we pay keen attention to the story, he had not yet set out on the journey to his father. Before he left to make his way back home, he settled the matter within himself. He acknowledged that he had sinned, not only against his father but also against heaven.

2. Humility

The act of genuine repentance is one that causes a person to be humble before God and ask for His forgiveness. His humility was put on full display when his heart's desire was to be a hired help in his father's house. He was aware that his sonly status was lost to him based on his actions and was willing to become a servant to survive. The harshness of his circumstances, coupled with his squandered inheritance, birthed in him a desire to serve. Serving in his father's house was his way of surviving the pain his external environment had exposed him to.

TIME TO MOVE!

In spite of all the internal dialogue and repentance that had taken place, Luke 15:19 finds him in the same place, looking at the pigs eating while he remained hungry. Sadly, I have been right here many times, looking at the bad relationship, the poor work choices, a lukewarm life, but though my circumstances had triggered me, and I was repentant in my heart, I did not move. I stayed stuck in the cycle, refusing to break free of my comfort zone. Restoring your relationship with God and your position as a daughter requires movement. This movement can take many forms, such as an actual movement to the altar, moving parishes or states, or moving into ministry, but the time to move is now. Luke 15:20 says he got up and went to his father. He took the road he had taken to leave his father to make his way back home.

Today, as we close, I share with you that it is time to start the journey back home. I urge you to remember the care, love, and provisions the Father's love brings. You do have a home, and God is wooing you back today. Take the first step to reflect on His goodness, repent in your heart, and then start the journey back home to a Father whose eyes are staring out into the distance, awaiting your arrival.

The Bible is clear that the prodigal son had a moment when his external circumstances and his pain triggered within him a moment of reflection and a realization that would change the trajectory of his life.

ACTIVATION #2

1. Can you identify a place of hunger or pain in your story?

2. Pray a prayer of repentance, taking responsibility, and asking God any questions you may have.

3. Make the decision today to come home.

Journey to the Father:

Changing of the Garment

TODAY'S SCRIPTURE: ZECHARIAH 3:1-10 AND LUKE 15:20–27

You may have been wondering how I missed out on what is the most incredible part of the prodigal son story. Not to worry; today we will pick up where we left off in our last reading. Today, we will be focusing on the father's response to his son's return, and what it means for us on our journey to the Father. Before I go on, it is important to highlight that repentance and reconciliation require us to actively participate.

We start today where we ended yesterday's reading in Luke 15:20, *"So he got up and went to his father. But while he was still a long way off, his father saw him and was filled with compassion for him, he ran to his son, threw his arms around him and kissed him." (NIV)*.

This verse is loaded with emotion and insight into the heart of the father towards his son. From this verse alone, we see:

1. The father was waiting in anticipation for his son's return.

2. His heart was one of compassion and not anger or condemnation.

3. He left his position to meet his son on the journey.

4. He embraced him despite his physical and emotional state.

This breakdown is a reminder today of why this book was written: the call of *Daughter, Come Home* echoes through the story as your heavenly Father is waiting eagerly for you to return home. His heart is to embrace, with compassion, His daughter who was lost and is now found.

Our time today will be pulling apart the other things that the father did once his son returned home. This will be instructive as to what we can expect or help us identify where we are on the journey.

Luke 15:22 says, *"But the father said to his servants…" (ESV).*

a. Bring the best robe and put it on him.

In the Bible, we have multiple examples of the attire of an individual being changed as they underwent transformation or were being promoted to a new level or season. We have Esther, who underwent a year of spices and grooming before meeting the king. We have Joseph, who, before he went before Pharaoh to interpret his dream, was washed and shaved. Changing clothes is symbolic of stripping away the old identity and embracing the new. Though changing clothes is easy to conceptualize, the process of renewing our identity can be a long and painful one as it requires a renewal of the mind, an intentional changing of behaviors, and the consistent study of the Word. As daughters of God, we are called a holy nation, a royal priesthood.

An even more vivid example of the changing of the garments can be found in Zechariah 3:3-4, *"Now Joshua (high priest) was dressed in filthy clothes as he stood before the angel. The angel said to those who were standing before him," Take off his filthy clothes." Then he said to Joshua, "See, I have taken away your sin and I will put fine garments on you."" (AMP).*

In this text, we see the angel of the Lord explaining clearly why the filthy garments were changed. It signified the removal of the sinful life, which for us under the new covenant has been purchased by the rich, red blood of Jesus.

In both stories, the prodigal son and Joshua the high priest, the changing of the garments was removed first, as something we should expect once repentance has occurred. The emphasis here is set to remind us that there is first a taking off and a stripping away of the old before the new garments are put in.

b. Put a ring on his finger.

The second element that the father instructed the servants to bring was the ring. The cultural context is critical in understanding the symbol of the ring. Research indicates that the ring given to the son was a family signet ring signaling a restoration of his authority as a son. Throughout scripture, we see rings being given as a means of access to power and authority. Prime examples are:

Then Pharaoh took his signet ring from his finger and put it on Joseph's finger. He dressed him in robes of fine linen and put a gold chain around his neck. (Genesis 41:42).

So the king took his signet ring from his hand and gave it to Haman the Agagite, the son of Hammedatha, the enemy of the Jews. (Esther 3:10 – ESV).

A most critical part of our journey will be the restoration of our authority. For the prodigal son, his symbol of authority was the ring, but when we journey into our accompanying story of Zechariah 3:5, the significant symbol of his authority was a turban.

Then I said I will put a clean turban on his head. So they put a clean turban on his head and clothed him while the angel of the Lord stood by. (Zechariah 3:5 – ESV).

The turban here represents a key part of his priestly garments, so the placing of the turban on his head was a key indicator of his restoration to his priestly anointing and office.

c. Sandals on his feet (identity and access).

This one was something I never thought of much, despite hearing the story so many times. However, as I thought about my own journey back to the Father, I was curious about the symbolism of the shoes. I discovered that the shoes were also tied to his identity as a son. Research revealed that in those times, slaves did not wear shoes, and it was possible he had returned home without shoes; a possible reflection of the hard times he had fallen on. The father asking for shoes was a clear indication of how he saw him and how he would be treated: as a son.

As we close today, I want to highlight a powerful observation of the father's attitude towards his lost son. The father was focused on aligning the son's identity and authority as one of his first actions. A son or daughter out of place is dangerous, so the father addressed that gap immediately.

As daughters, I also want us to see that our identity, authority, and access is in Him and through Him. John 15:5 shows our connection and total dependence on God, *"I am the vine; you are the branches. If you remain in me and I in you, you will bear much fruit; apart from me you can do nothing." (NIV).*

In studies of power and leadership, this is called "delegated authority," which means the source of the authority and power is outside of the person. Let us never forget that our connection to our Father is critical for our success.

On this journey back to the Father, be prepared to submit to the process of restoration and transformation of your identity and authority.

ACTIVATION #3

1. What symbol stood out the most in the prodigal story and why?

2. Can you identify any cracks in your identity that may need to be realigned?

Journey To The Father:

Know Your Enemy

TODAY'S READING: LUKE 22

Today, our journey back to the Father takes us to the foundation of our faith: the death and resurrection of our Lord and Savior Jesus Christ. His death, burial, and resurrection are the reason we have hope for repentance and restoration, and the reason we have an eternal hope after death. Our time today will be spent in Luke 22, looking at the decisions of two disciples and how they affected the trajectory of their destiny. I encourage you to pause here and spend some time going through Luke 22.

A LOOK AT TWO DISCIPLES

I took the liberty of pulling out some key scriptures just to deepen our understanding of our conversation today.

JUDAS

Then Satan entered Judas Iscariot, who was one of the twelve disciples, and he went to the leading priests and captains of the Temple guard to discuss the best way to betray Jesus to them. (Luke 22:3 – AMP).

But here at this table, sitting among us as a friend, is the man who will betray me. (Luke 22:21 – NLT).

But Jesus said, "Judas, would you betray the Son of Man with a kiss?" (Luke 22:48 – NLT).

SIMON PETER

"Simon, Simon, Satan has asked to sift each of you like wheat. But I have pleaded in prayer for you Simon, that your faith should not fail. So, when you have repented and turned to me again, strengthen your brother. (Luke 22:31 – NLT).

A servant girl noticed him in the firelight and began staring at him. Finally she said "This man was one of Jesus's follower's" But Peter denied it. (Luke 22:56 – NLT).

And Peter left the courtyard, weeping bitterly. (Luke 22:62 – NLT).

KEY OBSERVATIONS FROM THE DISCIPLES

God is not shocked by our mistakes or failures.

When I first started walking with God, I was on fire. I can recall being at university, and my first order of business was finding where the University College Christian Fellowship (UCCF) met. While my friends were busy experiencing university hall life and freedom from their parents, I was deep in dance rehearsal and any Christian activity I could participate in. Such a contrast from my early twenties, when I was lost and confused and seeking validation in the wrong places. One of the verses that has anchored me has been Luke 22:32, *"When you have repented, strengthen your brothers." (NLT)*. It communicated to me that God was aware of my falling away and was actively interceding on my behalf.

In Luke 22, Jesus took the time during the last supper to highlight that He was aware of both Peter's denial and Judas' betrayal, and He was not being taken by surprise. His omniscient nature as the God who knows all was on full display at this supper as He opened up to them things to come.

I want this to encourage you today as you reflect on your own journey with God. God is not shocked by your story or your journey. Our wounds, sins, and disappointments were known by Him, yet He died for us. Romans 8:29 reminds us that, *"For those whom he foreknew he also predestined to be conformed to the image of his Son, in order that he might be the firstborn among many brothers." (ESV)*. Let us take comfort in knowing that Jesus knows and is seated at the right hand of the Father, making intercession for us as He did for Peter.

We have a real enemy: be vigilant.

For the first time while writing this book, I noticed a commonality between Peter and Judas. Satan was present. Lurking in the background of the story, Luke tells us that Satan entered Judas and had a desire to sift Peter. I ask you to step back and look at the story of your life and see if you can identify where Satan was present, whether subtly or in your face.

1 Peter 5:8 says, *"Be alert and of a sober mind. Your enemy, the devil prowls around like a roaring lion for someone to devour." (NIV)*. Whether we are comfortable with the concept of an enemy or not, it does not negate his existence and his utter dislike for the children of God. Even at the end of Jesus's life, Satan was present, infiltrating His inner circle to get access to Him. I encourage us today to take the Bible's encouragement as a key in this season: *"Be alert and of a sober mind."* This requires us to stay in prayer, read the Word, recommit to Christian community, and serve others in some capacity. Satan

knew that Simon Peter was critical to God's plan to establish His kingdom here on earth. If he could be thoroughly sifted, his faith could be weakened, and it would impact the destiny of all connected. Let us never forget that the enemy's operations on the earth have not changed; he seeks to steal, kill, and destroy you and me. As you have made the decision to recommit your life to God, be vigilant.

Our response after a mistake or a fall matters.

A good man may fall seven times and rise again. (Proverbs 24:16 – NLT - paraphrased).

Both Judas and Peter made mistakes that ultimately impacted how we see them today. I want us to consider their response to their mistakes.

When Judas who betrayed Jesus, saw that Jesus was condemned, he was seized with remorse and returned the thirty pieces of silver to the chief priests and elders. So, Judas threw the money into the temple and left. Then he went away and killed himself. (Matthew 27:3-5).

I am going to fish, Simon Peter told them, and they said, "We'll go with you." So, they went out and got into the boat, but that night they caught nothing. (John 21:3 – NIV).

As we draw to a close today, I am taking the moment to reflect on my walk with God; the good, the bad, and the times I walked away and stopped believing.

- I was disappointed that I had let God down publicly, and the public shame became a prison.

- I resigned myself to feeling I was second best and stopped dreaming.

- I pulled away from the church community and found identity, community, and purpose in my job.

I was a lot like Peter as he went back to fishing, and he took others with him. We know from the text that he and his friends caught nothing. Many of us go back to what we know: our culture, our jobs, the old places and people that gave us comfort. My call for us today, however, is to keep faith alive.

Judas gave up all hope and killed himself after coming to the realization of what he had done, and Peter went back to his old life. Jesus had said to Peter, however, that He was praying for him that his faith would not fail—his faith in the God who chose him, who had a beautiful destiny for him, and who loved him dearly. Jesus' love for Peter had factored in his denial, so before Jesus ascended into heaven, he found Peter in his old spot.

I join with Jesus today, praying for you as you read this chapter that your faith would not fail.

ACTIVATION #4

1. Think about the fact that God already knew about your failure or mistake. How does it make you feel toward Him?

2. What area of your life do you need to experience the strengthening of your faith? Be reminded that Jesus is interceding for you.

The Journey To The Father:

Feed My Sheep

TODAY'S SCRIPTURE: LUKE 22:31

Today, as we close our time together, we will spend the time with Peter as our main character and model how the book was structured.

Our scriptures for the day will sandwich his life when Jesus was on earth, focusing on their first and last interactions together.

WHERE ARE YOU?

When we hear the name "Peter," there are so many thoughts and feelings that may be conjured up in our minds. However, the work of Apostle Peter has had an undeniable impact on the church to this day. Like us, however, Peter had an interesting journey, and today we look at a few of those. We will start with how Simon Peter became a disciple.

Luke 5 tells us that Jesus borrowed Simon's boat to allow Him to teach a group of people who were following Him. From this, Jesus directed Simon and the other fishermen to put their nets down again, though they initially protested, as their toiling all night and day was not the most conducive to catching fish, but they obeyed.

For he and all his companions were completely astounded at the catch of fish which they had taken; and so were James and John, sons of Zebedee, who were partners with Simon [Peter]. Jesus said to Simon, "Have no fear; from now on you will be catching men!" (Luke 5:9-11 - AMP).

We see men who, like us, had an encounter with Jesus and whose lives were changed. I can still recall the fire and love I felt when I first encountered God's presence. It is a season that cannot be described.

I invite you to join me in jogging your memory to recall your first experience with Jesus.

We see Simon Peter leaving his large catch of fish, his boat, and his skill to follow Jesus.

After they had brought their boats to land, they left everything and followed Him [becoming His disciples, believing and trusting in Him and following His example]. (Luke 5:11 - AMP).

We now head over to our second text for today, where we will observe Peter's last interaction with Jesus before He ascended to heaven. Join me in John 21:2-3, *"Simon Peter, and Thomas who is called Didymus (the twin), and Nathanael from Cana of Galilee, as well as [John and James] the sons of Zebedee, and two others of His disciples were together. Simon Peter said to them, "I am going fishing." They said, "And we are coming with you." So they went out and got into the boat; and that night they caught nothing." (AMP).*

As you read, did similarities jump out at you as they did for me?

John 21 is set after Peter denied Jesus, and Jesus had been resurrected and was making appearances before His ascension. We initially noticed a few things:

1. Peter's disappointment in himself led him back to where he felt safe and comfortable. Peter was found fishing after he was appointed as the rock on which the church would be built. He returned to the place that was familiar.

2. His community followed him. The sons of Zebebee (John and James) said, *"We are coming with you."* Despite how he felt, he had been elevated to a leader in their eyes, and they were following him back to where Jesus had delivered them from.

3. In both scenarios, the Bible said they caught nothing. Though Peter and those with him went back to what they knew, it yielded no fruit or results.

This leads us to answer for the last time: *"Where are we?"*

Have we taken the last few days to truly evaluate where we stand in relationship to our Father and our purpose? Have we, like Peter, gone back to habits, places, and people who no longer serve us? And, like Peter, it yielded no fruit.

THE HEART OF THE FATHER

In both of our texts under review, we notice the heart of the Father on full display through Jesus's heart.

1. **He met them where they were.**

I truly believe that Peter was facing an internal crisis and may have given up on the future that Jesus, the Messiah, had promised him. We meet him in John 21, back where Jesus first found him. It warmed my heart to realize that Jesus knew exactly where to find Peter and went to find him. It reminds me of the many times, while going through my daily life, I would hear a random song that would penetrate the wall of hurt that was around my bleeding heart, or I would be sitting at the back of a church service, and the sharpness of the preached Word of God would arrest me. Like Peter, He knows where we are, and His passionate love will come chasing us down.

2. **He addressed their physical need.**

In both scenarios (see John 21:5-6, Luke 5:4-6), the men had toiled all night and caught nothing, and Jesus addressed their need in the moment. Jesus puts on full display that He cares about all our basic needs and about the things that concern us. He first ensured that the men with Peter achieved the task that was directly before them: catching fish. His instruction to put down their net was met with immediate obedience and overwhelming results.

3. **He called them to higher purposes.**

Another similarity, and the one that will form the basis of most of our time spent together today, is His call into divine purpose. On His first encounter with Simon, He reframes his identity and gives them a glimpse of their new purpose.

And so was also James, and John, the sons of Zebedee, which were partners with Simon. And Jesus said unto Simon, Fear not; from henceforth thou shalt catch men. (Luke 5:10 – KJV).

In His last encounter with Peter, he may have expected a scolding, but Jesus had come to remind Peter of who he was and the call on his life. I am here to remind you that your mistakes do not erase His love for you or the call on your life. After this call, the Holy Spirit would descend, and the church as we know it was born.

FEED MY SHEEP

As we draw our days together to a close, we will end by examining the last words Jesus said to Peter before He ascended into heaven, and I pray they echo in your heart as they did in mine. Peter, like us, has a critical part to play in the building of the kingdom. Let us take a look at this life-changing encounter:

When they had finished breakfast, Jesus said to Simon Peter, "Simon, son of John, do you love me more than these?" He said to him, "Yes, Lord; you know that I love you." He said to him, "Feed my lambs." He said to him a second time, "Simon, son of John, do you love me?" He said to him, "Yes, Lord; you know that I love you." He said to him, "Tend my sheep." He said to him the third time, "Simon, son of John, do you love me?" Peter was grieved because he said to him the third time, "Do you love me?" and he said to him, "Lord, you know everything; you know that I love you." Jesus said to him, "Feed my sheep." (John 21:15-17 – ESV).

LOVE IS THE REASON FOR SERVING

I must admit that I grew up in a church where serving was taught to us as a basic Christian discipline, so I remember always being involved in some ministry of some kind. However, as the Holy

Spirit led me to the focus of the final section of the book, I came across a story and an encounter I had never read before: the restoration of Simon Peter before we see him in the book of Acts. It highlighted two main points that brought so much conviction that I have taken action, even as I write to you today.

Jesus asked Peter three times, *"Do you love Me?"* (the same number of times he denied Him). For each of the responses, God highlighted that the appropriate response for loving Him was serving others in some capacity. We serve because we love Him. Our service is out of a deep love for who He is and what He has done for us. It is not an act of compulsion but an act of love.

He gave Peter three specific groups of people to focus on during their last encounter:

1. ***"Yes, Lord; you know that I love you." He said to him, "Feed my lambs."***

Lambs are young sheep that are under a year old. Jesus' call for Peter to feed them draws immediate focus to the young believer and walking alongside them to develop an understanding of the Word, their identity in Christ, sanctification, and consecration.

2. ***Yes, Lord; you know that I love you." He said to him, "Tend my sheep."***

We see a progression of the believer's journey as though they are no longer referred to as lambs and are now in the journey of maturing. Peter is called to tend to them as a shepherd would his sheep. Jesus was calling him, and us by extension, to serve the body of Christ by maturing to leadership to be able to provide guidance, support, and leadership to the body.

3. *Peter was grieved because he said to him the third time, "Do you love me?" and he said to him, "Lord, you know everything; you know that I love you." Jesus said to him, "Feed my sheep."*

Jesus then goes back to the feeding of the sheep, which He intentionally separates from "tending to," emphasizing the need for spiritual food on a continuous basis for the growth of the believer and the sheep.

We have all been called to the kingdom to serve others, and this reminds us of the heart of the Father. It was always for people and their growth in Him.

We are called to serve the kingdom. Today, I welcome you back home as we co-labour in the kingdom together.

ACTIVATION #5

1. Can you identify what represents the boat you have gone back to after pain or disappointment in life?

2. Where do you feel called to "Feed My sheep?"

ABOUT THE AUTHOR

An extrovert with introverted rhythms, Jodianna is a storyteller at heart whose love for words was kindled early—winning national essay and reading competitions by age ten. A lifelong book lover, her first birthday cake was shaped like a book, a fitting symbol for a life shaped by story. From Enid Blyton to Lorna Goodison, literature fueled her voice and passion. With professional roots spanning communication and HR across industries, she brings a unique blend of creativity, empathy, and vulnerability to her writing. Her first fictional piece, *One an Drive*, earned a winning spot in Hodder Education's Island Voices—Caribbean Contemporary Classics series. *Daughter, Come Home* is her debut devotional, a heartfelt invitation for daughters of God to rediscover intimacy with the Father.